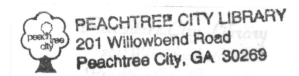

MOTHER TERESA

Richard Tames

Franklin Watts
New York • London • Sydney • Toronto

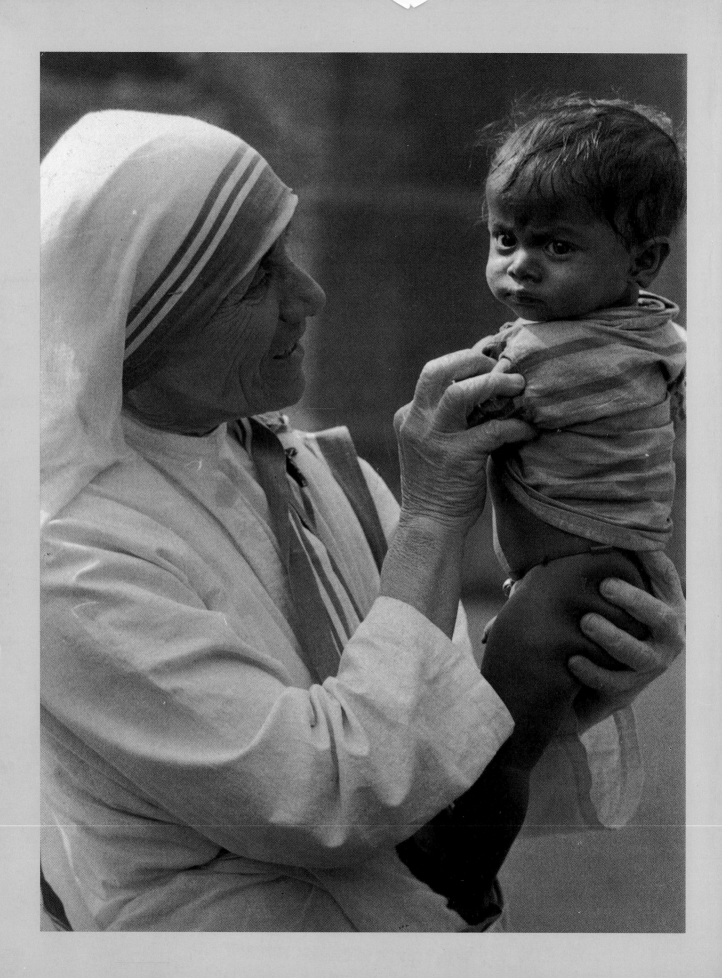

Contents

© 1989 Franklin Watts

First published in the USA by
Franklin Watts Inc.
387 Park Avenue South
New York
N.Y. 10016

Phototypeset by: JB Type, Hove, East Sussex.
Printed in: Belgium
Series Editor: Penny Horton
Designed by: Ross George
Illustrated by: Malcolm Walker

Tames, Richard.
    Mother Teresa/Richard Tames.
        p. cm — (Lifetimes)
    Includes index.
    Summary: A biography of the nun who founded the Missionary Sisters
and Brothers of Charity and gained wide recognition for her work
with the destitute and dying in Calcutta and other places. She was
awarded the Nobel Peace Prize in 1979.
    ISBN 0-531-10847-3
    1. Teresa, Mother, 1910–   – Juvenile literature. 2. Missionaries
of Charity – Biography – Juvenile literature. (1. Teresa, Mother,
1910–   . 2. Nuns. 3. Missionaries. 4. Missionaries of Charity.)
I. Title. II. Series: Lifetimes (London, England)   89-9039
BX4406.5.Z8T35 1990   [B]   CIP
271'.97 – dc20   (92)   AC

The Call to Faith

Mother Teresa is one of the most famous names in the world. But, she was actually born with the name Ganxhe Agnes Bojaxhiu in Skopje, in the small kingdom of Serbia which is now a part of Yugoslavia.

Agnes, the third child of the Bojaxhiu family, was born in 1910. At the time, her sister, Aga, was seven and her brother, Lazar, four.

Agnes' father, Kole, was a rich merchant and a clever businessman with many interests. He sold medicines, built houses, imported goods from Italy and traveled widely, thrilling his children with stories of foreign places. He was a loving father and took a strong interest in his children's lessons, always urging them to work hard.

Mother Teresa in the distinctive blue-edged sari of the Missionaries of Charity.

A picturesque square in the Turkish part of Skopje in Yugoslavia, the town where Mother Teresa was born in 1910.

Kole Bojaxhiu was also a public-spirited man who built Skopje's first theater, gave generously to the Church, fed the poor at his own table and set an example of service to the community. When Agnes was just eight, he was taken ill very suddenly at a meeting of the city council and died the next day. Great crowds came to his funeral and, according to custom, every child was given a handkerchief to dry their tears and remember him by.

Kole's sudden death left Agnes's mother, Drana, with the task of bringing up three children alone. She was unable to keep up her husband's business, so she used her needlework skills to make fine clothes.

But although the family was no longer wealthy, Drana still continued her husband's generous ways, giving food and help to the poor and old. The power of this example of practical Christianity stayed with Agnes throughout her life, as she later recalled:–

"Many of the poor in and around Skopje knew our house and none left it empty-handed. We had guests at our table every day. At first I used to ask, 'Who are they?' and Mother would answer 'Some are relatives, but all of them are our people.' When I was older I realized that the strangers were poor people who had nothing and whom my mother was feeding."

The Bojaxhiu family prayed together every day, celebrated all the religious festivals, and made a pilgrimage each year to the shrine of the Madonna of Letnice in the mountains of Montenegro.

As a young child, Agnes was often ill. Confined to bed, she developed a passion for reading which helped her to become a top pupil at school.

As a teenager, Agnes became a leading member of a religious society for young Catholic girls, which organized walks, lectures and meetings. At some of these meetings the members heard about the work of Catholic **missionaries** in foreign countries and organized collections to support their work.

Montenegro, a beautiful setting for the shrine of the Madonna of Letnice.

Thanks to Drana's tireless efforts, her children made good progress. Aga went to study at a commercial college and Lazar won a scholarship to study for a year in Austria, going on to the Military Academy in Tirana, capital of Albania. Agnes, meanwhile, began to set her heart on a very different career — as a missionary.

Although Drana was a firm Christian who felt proud that Agnes wanted to become a nun, she also knew how hard it was for a girl to give up her chance of marriage and a family of her own. It would be even more difficult for her to become a missionary, as it would mean leaving behind her country, family and friends as well. Drana wanted to be sure that Agnes had the strength she would need and told her:–

"My daughter, if you begin something, begin it with your whole heart. Otherwise, don't begin it at all."

After years of prayer, Agnes finally decided to ask her priest how she could get to India as a missionary. She was told to join the Order of Loreto nuns in Ireland, who worked in the Bengal area of India, around the vast city of Calcutta.

When Agnes's brother, Lazar, heard of her plans he wrote to her to try to persuade her not to leave. But she wrote back:–

"You think you are important, because you are an officer, serving a king of two million subjects. But I am serving the King of the whole world. Which of us do you think is in the better place?"

Agnes Bojaxhiu left Skopje in September 1928 with another Yugoslav girl, Betika Kajnc. They traveled across Austria, Switzerland and France, passing through London before finally arriving in Ireland. It was a great journey for someone who had never left her own country before.

During her stay in Ireland, Agnes began to learn about the Loreto Order and to master the English language. She also changed her name to Sister Mary Teresa of the Child Jesus.

The route taken by Agnes Bojaxhiu and Betika Kajnc from Skopje to the Loreto Order in Ireland.

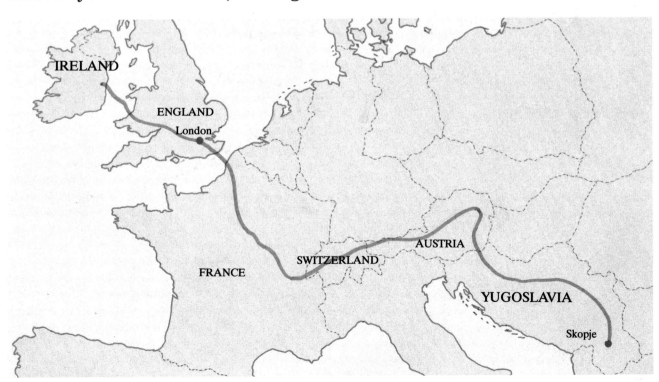

The Loreto Order

The Loreto Sisters are the Irish branch of the Institute of the Blessed Virgin Mary, an order of nuns founded in 1609 by a Yorkshirewoman called Mary Ward. Unlike other nuns Mary Ward's sisters did not live shut away from the world in a convent but obtained special permission from the Church to go out and work among the poor. Later Mary Ward opened schools in Rome and London. She died in York in 1645.

Forty years later a convent of the Institute was founded at York. Over the next century many Irish girls came to study there. In 1822 the Archbishop of Dublin gave the sisters Rathfarnham House as a headquarters in Ireland. They changed its name to Loreto Abbey, after the town in Italy famed for its Santa Casa (Holy House).

The Loreto Order was very successful in Ireland and grew rapidly. In 1841 it was asked to establish a foundation in Calcutta, India, where it set up schools and medical services. Nowadays over 7,000 children are still taught by Loreto Sisters.

Mother Teresa's Missionaries of Charity, following the example of the Loreto Order, was founded in 1950 to teach and care for the poor and sick in Calcutta.

The Call to Teach

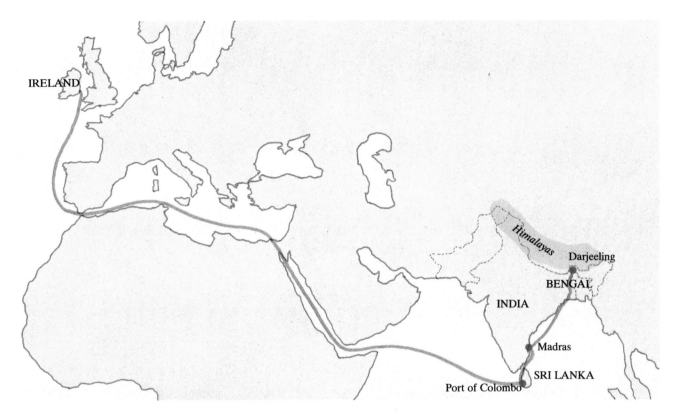

The young Sister Mary Teresa left for India on December 1, 1928 in the company of Betika Kajnc. Two days after Christmas their ship docked in Colombo, the great port of what is now Sri Lanka. The newcomer described her first impressions in a letter — "great poverty" amid lush tropical growth; "The whole city looked like an enormous garden." But Madras, one of India's three largest cities, deeply shocked her:–

" ... indescribable poverty ... Many families live in the streets ... Day and night they live in the open on mats they have made from large palm leaves — or, often, on bare ground. They are all virtually naked, wearing at best a ragged loincloth."

A second journey – from Ireland to India.

The two girls finally landed in Bengal on January 6, 1929 and set off for Darjeeling, in the foothills of the Himalayas. There, they spent a two year **novitiate**, learning the traditions of the Loreto Order in India, before taking the vows that would commit them for life. They also worked hard at learning languages.

A missionary who saw them at this time declared them to be "Really happy and fulfilled." They were very healthy and were making excellent progress in their language studies — "Already they are speaking English and Hindi well, and they are learning Bengali ... "

Left: **Some of the 100,000 people sleeping on the pavements of Calcutta.**

Below left: **The mountain resort of Darjeeling is also famed for its tea plantations.**

In Darjeeling Sister Teresa worked as a teacher at the Loreto Convent School, but she also spent part of her time in a charity hospital, where the constant flow of patients with terrible sores and ulcers reminded her of the misery and filth which blighted the lives of the poor.

Soon after taking her first vows in 1931 Sister Teresa left Darjeeling for the teeming city of Calcutta where she was assigned to teach at St. Mary's High School in the Entally district, an ugly place consisting of dirty factories and slums. Within this chaos stood the Loreto convent, neat and clean behind its high walls, with beautiful gardens and well-kept buildings, including St. Mary's, where Teresa would teach history and geography to girls from wealthy Bengali families.

But Teresa's endless appetite for work took her far beyond her regular duties as a teacher:—

"Apart from the school I have to care for many of the sick and help ten nuns in their studies ... And I have taken on another task: the school of St. Teresa which is also in Calcutta."

This was a very different sort of school. The first thing Teresa had to do was clean it up — a lesson in itself for some of her pupils:—

"I rolled up my sleeves immediately, rearranged the whole

room, found water and a broom and began to sweep the floor. This greatly astonished them. They had never seen a schoolmistress start lessons like that … and they stood staring at me for a long time. Seeing me cheerful and smiling, the girls began to help me and the boys brought me more water. After two hours that room was at least in part transformed into a clean schoolroom."

The room was divided into five separate classes and the number of pupils rose from 50 to nearly 400. Teresa was saddened by the children's poverty but inspired by their warmth toward her:–

"When I first saw where the children slept and ate, I was full of anguish. It is not possible to find worse poverty … when we first met, they were not at all joyful. They began to leap and sing only when I had put my hand on each dirty little head. From that day on they called me 'Ma' which means 'Mother'."

On Sundays, which was meant to be a day of rest and prayer, Mother Teresa visited her pupils at home:–

" … each family has a single room, two meters long and a meter-and-a-half wide. The doors are so narrow I can scarcely squeeze through them, the ceiling so low it is impossible to stand erect … I am no longer surprised that my pupils love their schools so much, nor that so many are ill … "

In 1937 Mother Teresa took her final vows as a nun. Immediately afterward she took over as the principal of St. Mary's School.

Above: **A time for God – Mother Teresa and her sisters at prayer.**

Left: **Giving them a sense of direction – Mother Teresa with her pupils.**

Calcutta

A hundred years ago the English poet Rudyard Kipling wrote a famous description of Calcutta, which he called the "City of Dreadful Night." A hundred years before him, when the great trading city was still young, an Englishwoman wrote that it was:—

"As awkward a place as can be conceived; and so very irregular that it looks as if all the houses had been thrown up in the air and fallen down again by accident as they now stand … a confusion of very superb and very shabby houses, dead walls, straw huts, warehouses and I know not what."

When Mother Teresa arrived in Calcutta 150 years after that passage was written, the city was as bewildering as ever and the contrasts between wealth and poverty as great. The difference was that it was now on a gigantic scale, for the city had swollen to a population of more than two million.

Calcutta – a major industrial city where cows wander the streets and people wash in gutters.

The Call to Serve

For nine years Mother Teresa plunged herself into her work as headmistress. St. Mary's must have seemed like an island of calm and kindness in a world of turmoil and danger. The outbreak of World War II (1939–45) brought with it the threat of a Japanese invasion of India. This was followed by a great famine which devastated Bengal and cost hundreds of thousands of lives. Even when the war ended there was no certainty of peace for India. It was clear that Britain had been exhausted by six years of fighting and could hold on to her great colony no longer. India would soon become an independent country. But the leaders of Indian independence could not agree on how the country should be run. Riots, perhaps even a civil war, seemed inevitable.

Through these dark times Mother Teresa returned again and again in her thoughts and prayers to the words of a missionary in India which she had first heard when she was a young girl in Skopje:–

"Each person has a road to follow that is his own, and he must follow that road."

Mother Teresa with a group of her older pupils. Many were to follow her example of service.

Left: **Mother Teresa in church. Daily worship is an important part of her routine.**

Below: **Dressed in a discarded sack, this child begs from passers-by.**

On September 10, 1946 Mother Teresa found a new turning in her road. Once a year she went back to Darjeeling, where she had served her novitiate, for a period of rest and prayer. September 10, is now celebrated by her followers as "Inspiration Day" as a result of her ordinary, but momentous journey on that date:–

"I was traveling to Darjeeling by train, when I heard the voice of God … I was sure it was God's voice. I was certain that he was calling me. The message was clear: I must leave the convent to help the poor by living among them. This was a command, something to be done, something definite. I knew where I had to be. But I did not know how to get there."

When she came back to Calcutta, Mother Teresa spoke to Archbishop Perier, the head of the Catholic Church in that area and the local representative of the Pope. The

archbishop cautiously listened to this new idea for an order of nuns to work among the poor. Any such project would need careful thought at the best of times, but with India in the grip of a political fever Calcutta might be invaded by hordes of **refugees** at any time. He was therefore uncertain it would be wise to send unprotected nuns out onto the streets in such circumstances.

It took a year for the archbishop to decide to bless the venture and ask Rome for permission to go ahead. Mother Teresa herself had to write to the head of the Loreto Order in Ireland for permission to leave its ranks. Permission was granted and the Pope in Rome gave his blessing for her bold new plan. On August 16, 1948, a year after India became an independent country, Mother Teresa made her own declaration of independence and left the convent at Entally for the last time, setting out on the path that would take her to the poorest of the poor.

First, she traveled to Patna, 385 kilometers (240 miles) from Calcutta. Having helped out in hospitals and clinics for many years Mother Teresa had valuable nursing experience. But she had never had any formal medical training.

At Patna, on the banks of the great River Ganges, an American group of Medical Missionary Sisters ran a hospital and outpatient department, where the poor could come for free treatment. Here, Mother Teresa underwent intensive training for four months. She also discussed her plan for a new order of nuns with Mother Dengal, the Patna hospital's surgeon. When Mother Teresa declared that her nuns would eat only rice and salt, so that they would be even worse off than the poor they had come to help, Mother Dengal quickly changed Mother Teresa's mind.

"Do you want to help the poor and the sick, or do you want to die with them? Do you want your young nuns to lose their lives, or do you want them healthy and strong, so they can work for Christ?"

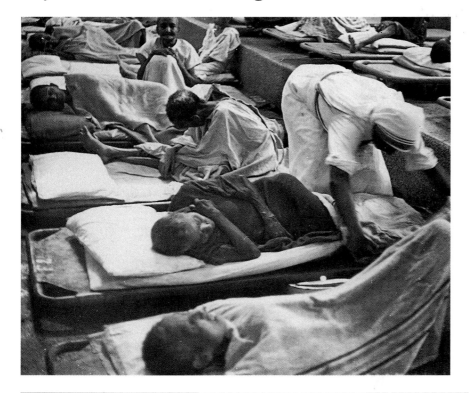

Mother Teresa – a relentless nurse – tends to patients with care and efficiency.

When she returned to Calcutta in December 1948, Mother Teresa found the city flooded with refugees. India had achieved its independence, but not as one country. The areas where **Muslims** made up the majority of the population became the separate country of Pakistan. Many **Hindus** fled across the new border to avoid living in a country run by Muslims. When they arrived in Calcutta they simply camped out wherever they could. At this time Mother Teresa showed her own commitment to the new independent nation by becoming an Indian citizen.

Mother Teresa began her work in a small hut in a slum called Motijhil, right next to the Entally convent. Here she gathered together five local children and began to teach them how to read, write and keep themselves clean.

Each day more children arrived.

Soon she began to give out prizes for progress and, at midday, she would give them milk. Gradually word of her work began to spread. At first she taught the children by writing letters in the dust on the floor. So someone gave her a blackboard. Someone else gave the school chairs. Gradually she began to attract a band of supporters, including some of the girls she had taught at the Entally convent.

The first of these was Subhasini Das, the daughter of a wealthy Bengali family. She became the first sister of the new order, which was to be called the Congregation of the Missionaries of Charity. She chose the name Sister Agnes, as a tribute to Mother Teresa's own name.

By May 1949 there were three sisters and by November, there were five. In the autumn of 1950 there were 12 sisters and the order was formally established.

The order had its own distinctive habit — a white sari, like those worn by the poor, bordered in blue, with a small crucifix on the left shoulder. Each nun had two saris, one pair of sandals, underwear, a rope girdle, a crucifix, a mattress and a bucket to wash themselves and their clothes. They begged for food and anything else they were given was given directly to the poor.

Bewildered and exhausted, these refugees from Pakistan camp out in Calcutta's Sealdah station. They are out of danger, but what future do they have?

Bengal and Bengali

Bengal is the densely populated region of northeastern India which was conquered by the British in 1757. Nowadays Bengal is divided into two parts. The western part, mostly Hindu in religion, makes up the Indian state of West Bengal. The eastern part, mostly Muslim, was the Eastern Province of Pakistan from 1947 to 1971, but since then has become the independent state of Bangladesh.

Bengal is a flat land with a heavy rainfall. Sometimes this enables the farmers to produce large supplies of rice and fish. However, at other times the climate can lead to disastrous floods which destroy crops and leave many homeless.

Bengali, the main language of this region, is the national language of Bangladesh, which has a population of over 100 million. It is also the state language of West Bengal, which has a population of about 60 million, and is widely spoken in the neighboring states of Bihar, Orissa and Assam. In all, perhaps 200 million people speak Bengali. It is one of India's 16 official languages.

Bengal, a nation divided by religion. West Bengal, mostly Hindu and Bangladesh, mostly Muslim.

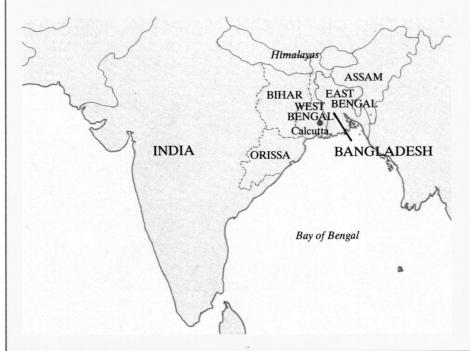

The Mission to Care

It was clear that if the work of the Missionaries of Charity was to progress, and reach more people in need, a bigger building would be essential. It would have to house a growing number of sisters, provide a place where others could be trained, store food and medicines, and provide shelter for the desperate.

Thanks to Mother Teresa's good friend, Father Henry, she found out about a wealthy Muslim who was going to leave Calcutta to live in Pakistan. He was willing to accept a low price for his big house in the center of town and Archbishop Perier quickly found the money to pay for it. Thus, 54a Lower Circular Road was soon established as the official headquarters, the "Mother House," of Mother Teresa's Missionaries of Charity.

When she first saw her new building Mother Teresa said to Father Henry, "it is too big, what will we do with all that?" But he replied, "Mother, you will need it all. There will come a day when you will ask where you can put all your people." He was soon to be proved right. Over the next few years Mother Teresa searched for more buildings all over the city.

The sisters treated the poor where they found them, which was mostly on the streets. The hospitals were full of those who could afford to pay for them and they had no room for those who could not. Mother Teresa began to see the need for a special

The headquarters and main office of the Missionaries of Charity.

building, a place where the dying could die in peace.

One day Mother Teresa found an old woman dying on the steps of a hospital. The woman was too weak even to brush away the rats and insects that were starting to eat her feet. Mother Teresa went inside and argued with the hospital officials until they found a bed for the woman so that she could die peacefully. Then she went straight to the town hall to demand help in finding a building for such people to go to. The officials at the town hall offered her a run down pilgrims' hostel behind a temple devoted to Kali, the Hindu goddess of death, where many Hindus already went to die. The Missionaries of Charity moved in the next day.

The Home for the Dying **Destitute** began to take in people immediately and was officially opened in August 1952. It was called Nirmal Hriday — the Place of the Pure Heart.

Unfortunately, some local people became angry about the new home for the dying. They thought that the sisters were just trying to help Hindus so that they could convert them to Christianity before they died. Some of the nuns were pelted with sticks and stones by angry local people. Finally the protests reached the chief of the city police who came himself to see the sisters. When he saw the work that Mother Teresa and her helpers were doing he told the protestors that he would clear the nuns out of their building on one condition, "that you get your own mothers and sisters to do the work that she is doing."

Even though the police approved of the sisters' work their problems continued until, one day, Mother Teresa found a young man lying ill outside the temple of Kali. He was

Below: **Bamboo and matting shelters provide a temporary home.**

Right: **Safe haven – a crippled beggar outside Nirmal Hriday.**

Shishu (children) Bhavan (House) in 1962. Note the line of clean washing on the roof.

dying of **cholera** and everyone was afraid to touch him. But, Mother Teresa carried him away to Nirmal Hriday and took care of him until he died. Later she found out that he was a Hindu priest from the temple, a leader of the people who had been against her. When the local people saw how she had cared for him they understood at last that the Missionaries of Charity had come to help everyone, regardless of their religion.

Mother Teresa wanted to love the dying, but she also wanted to help the living, and especially those who might otherwise die. She knew that many babies were born to mothers who were too poor or too ill to feed them. Sometimes these babies were simply left to die on rubbish dumps. Whenever an abandoned baby was found, the Missionaries of Charity would take it home and care for it. In 1955 Mother Teresa opened Shishu Bhavan, a special home for abandoned babies. Soon police and other officials began to send unwanted infants there from all

over the city. Some came too late, but others were saved to grow up healthy and happy.

Another affliction that concerned Mother Teresa greatly was leprosy. It is a terrible disease which takes a number of forms but basically destroys the human body bit by bit, often making the victim both helpless and hideous. Because it can be infectious people have always kept away from lepers, forcing them to live and die with only each other for company.

In 1957 Mother Teresa set up a shelter for lepers at Gobra, on the outskirts of Calcutta. It was an important step forward but only a small one as Gobra could only house about 150 lepers and Calcutta was believed to have as many as 50,000.

In the same year a **dispensary** was opened at Shishu Bhavan, where 600 lepers could obtain modern drugs which could help to control the disease. A Leprosy Fund was also organized to hold street collections to help pay for medicines.

The shelter at Gobra soon had to be closed down to release the land for building. When Mother Teresa went to look at another possible site a crowd drove her away with sticks and stones because they were afraid to have lepers living near them. But only a few weeks later a large company gave her a generous sum for her work, an American charity sent her an ambulance and Dr. Sen, a leading Indian leprosy expert, retired from his hospital job and offered to work with her without pay. With these three strokes of good fortune she was able to set up her first mobile leprosy clinic.

Soon after that, a Methodist minister at Barrackpore, an industrial area on the outskirts of the city, offered land for a lepers' settlement. This place, now known as Titigarh, became not only a home and treatment center but also a training school where those who were less badly afflicted could learn to help themselves and others by making their own clothes, shoes and bandages. Again Mother Teresa showed how despair could be turned into hope and even when hope failed, there would always be love.

Above: **A sister giving out medicines and advice at a dispensary.**

Left: **Titigarh lepers' settlement. The Bengali slogan says "Touch the leper with your love."**

Leprosy

Leprosy is an infectious disease that can cause severe damage to the skin and the nerves that control our sense of touch. The disease usually leads to light spots on the skin which may then turn into hard raised lumps. Later on there may be a weakening of the muscles and even paralysis. If it is not controlled the disease can lead to the loss of fingers, toes and other parts of the body.

Nowadays there are drugs that can stop the disease developing, as long as it is detected in its early stages, and make it much less likely to spread to others. There are still about five million infected individuals around the world today, almost all in poor, tropical countries.

A sister helps a fingerless leper open a matchbox.

The Mission to the World

In 1964 Pope Paul VI visited India. While he was there he drove around in a white Lincoln Continental, presented to him by Notre Dame University, South Bend, Indiana. It was one of the most expensive cars in the world and as he prepared to leave India he gave it to Mother Teresa, knowing she would find a way to put it to good use.

By now she had many helpers in all walks of life. Whenever she needed an expert to advise her she could usually count on someone to spare her the time. Most were in India but some were abroad, spreading news of her work, sending money and supplies or just praying for her success. Wherever they were, she called them her "Co-Workers." It was a group of these co-workers who helped her dispose of the Pope's car by organizing a raffle, with the car as first prize. The raffle raised a great deal of money for her work — five times what the car itself was worth at the time.

Mother Teresa encouraging the sick and hungry to accept free food.

A big welcome for Mother Teresa at one of her leprosy hospitals.

Mother Teresa was already building a special new settlement for 400 leper families on land given to her by the Indian government about 140 kilometers (90 miles) from Calcutta. She had decided to call it Shanti Nagar — the Place of Peace. Thirty houses were already going up. With the money from the car raffle she could now build a new hospital as well.

Shanti Nagar was dedicated to the idea that lepers should try to help themselves as much as possible, and so live life as fully as possible. From the beginning they learned to make their own bricks to build their own cottages. Then they went on to grow their own rice and raise their own cattle. They even set up their own printing press.

Until 1960 Mother Teresa had found more than enough to do in and around Calcutta. But as her work grew, her fame spread, although she

never sought to spread it herself. More and more often she was asked to send sisters to work in other parts of India and as her new order had survived successfully for a full ten years she was at last granted permission to expand. She now had over 100 sisters to help her do so.

In Delhi, the nation's capital, Prime Minister Nehru himself came to open her new children's home and in the great port city of Bombay she established a home for the dying destitute. When the Philippine government gave her the Magsaysay Award for International Understanding in 1962, the first of many foreign honors that were to be showered upon her, she used the prize money to build a children's home in Agra, about 200 kilometers (120 miles) southeast of Delhi.

In 1963 an Order of Missionary Brothers was established to work in areas where it was difficult for women to go. In 1965 the sisters and brothers were given permission to work outside India itself, in any country that might invite them. The first was Venezuela in South America, that year. In 1967 they went to Sri Lanka; in 1968 to Tanzania and in the same year, at the invitation of the Pope, to Rome to work among Sicilian **immigrants**, many of whom were unemployed and homeless. In 1969 Australia was added to their field of operations and in 1970 Jordan and England.

1970 was to be a year of reminders for Mother Teresa, now 60 years of age. The Yugoslav Red Cross invited her back to her birthplace as an honored guest. She returned to Skopje for the first time in 42 years. Many things must have seemed changed to her, especially since an earthquake in 1963 had virtually destroyed the city in which she had grown up. The visit to Skopje was Mother Teresa's first trip out of India for many years but her travels were only just beginning.

Above: **Heavy work with a light heart. Sisters loading supplies.**

Left: **Skopje, almost wiped out by Yugoslavia's worst ever earthquake.**

Nobel Prizes

Alfred Nobel (1833–96) was a Swedish industrialist who invented dynamite and made a great deal of money out of the manufacture of explosives. In his will he left most of his vast wealth to establish annual awards to the men and women who gave the greatest benefit to mankind in the fields of physics, chemistry, medicine, literature and peace.

The first four categories are decided by committees of learned Swedish professors, but the peace prize is awarded by a committee of the Norwegian government, the Storting. The award consists of a gold medal, a diploma and a gift of money. The first ever peace prize was awarded in 1901 to Henri Dunant, the Swiss founder of the Red Cross. Other winners have included the United States' Presidents, Theodore Roosevelt and Woodrow Wilson, the scientists Albert Schweitzer and Andrei Sakharov, the Swedish diplomat Dag Hammarskjöld and the civil rights campaigner, Martin Luther King. Mother Teresa was the third woman to be awarded the Nobel Peace Prize.

The Chairman of the Norwegian Nobel Committee presents Mother Teresa with the Peace Prize.

The Mission Continues

In the 1970s Mother Teresa became a world figure to rank beside presidents and prime ministers. Morarji Desai, India's Prime Minister at the time, wrote of her:–

"Many great people have trod this earth, but very few of these have been good people. Mother Teresa is good as well as great."

Honors for her work came flooding in. In 1971 she was awarded no less than three — the Pope John XXIII Peace Prize, the Good Samaritan Award and the Joseph P. Kennedy Foundation Award. In 1972 her adopted country, India, gave her the Jawaharlal Nehru Award for International Understanding. In 1973 the Duke of Edinburgh praised her as the first person to receive the Templeton Award for "Progress in Religion":–

"The sheer goodness which shines through Mother Teresa's life and work can only inspire **humility**, wonder and admiration — and what more is there to be said when the deeds speak so loudly for themselves?"

In 1979 Mother Teresa received the most prestigious prize of them all — the Nobel Peace Prize. When she went to Oslo, the Norwegian capital, to receive her award she told the prize committee:–

"Personally I am unworthy. I accept in the name of the poor because I believe that by giving me the prize they have recognized the presence of the poor in the world."

A time of joy and recognition. Mother Teresa happily answers reporters' questions on her return from Norway where she was awarded the Nobel Peace Prize.

There was a service of thanksgiving in the city's Lutheran Cathedral and a candlelit procession. But the celebration banquet in her honor was cancelled at her request and the money it would have cost was sent to India for the poor and the lepers. There was also $70,000 raised for the same cause by the young people of Norway and the official prize check, presented to her by King Olaf, for $190,000.

By the 1980s Mother Teresa had become a legend. In 1982 she went to war-torn Beirut as the special **envoy** of Pope John Paul II and rescued children from the rubble of a camp to place them in the safety of a home she herself had founded two years earlier. In 1984, when a gas leak at a chemical plant at Bhopal in India killed over 2,000 people and injured 20,000 more, Mother Teresa was there to comfort the victims. In 1988 she flew to Armenia in the bitter cold of winter to visit the survivors of the earthquake which destroyed three cities.

At the time of writing she is almost 80 years old and her mission to the world continues.

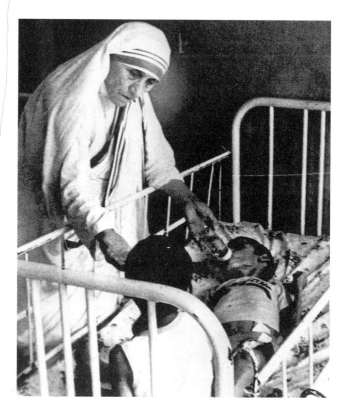

Above: **Mother Teresa offers food and comfort to wounded, frightened children in East Beirut.**

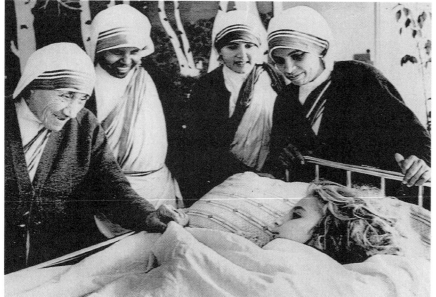

Left: **Mother Teresa in Armenia, with sisters who volunteered to nurse the injured.**

Messages from Mother Teresa

The Poverty of the Missionaries of Charity

"Desirous to share Christ's own poverty and that of our poor:

We accept to have everything in common and to share with one another in the Society.

We do not accept anything whatsoever from our parents, friends or benefactors for our personal use. Whatever is given to us is handed over to our superiors for the common use of the community or for the work.

We shall eat the food of the people, of the country where we live, using what is cheapest. It should be sufficient and wholesome so as to maintain good health which is essential for the work of our vocation.

Our houses shall be simple and modest, places where the poor feel at home.

We shall walk whenever opportunity offers, in order to take the cheapest means of transportation available.

We shall sleep in common dormitories without privacy like the poor.

We and our poor will depend entirely on Divine Providence both for our material and spiritual needs."

On Poverty Amidst Wealth

"In England … in Melbourne, in New York, we find lonely people who are known only by the number of their room. Why are we not there? Do we really know that there are people like this, maybe next door to us? Maybe there is a blind man who would be happy if you would read the newspaper for him. Maybe there is a rich person who has no one to visit him — he has plenty of other things, he is nearly drowning in them, but he needs your touch … Let us not be satisfied with just giving money. Money is not enough, they need your hearts to love them. So spread love everywhere you go: first of all in your own home."

Find Out More ...

Important Books

For the Brotherhood of Man Under the Fatherhood of God by K Spink (Colour Library International, 1981). An illustrated account of the work of the Missionaries of Charity.

Mother Teresa by M Craig (Hamish Hamilton, 1983). A brief illustrated biography.

Mother Teresa: Contemplative at the Heart of the World by A Devananda (Collins, Fount Paperbacks, 1985). A selection from the writings of Mother Teresa, introduced by a priest and admirer.

Mother Teresa: Her People and Her Work by D Doig (Collins, Fount Paperbacks, 1978). A biography by an Indian journalist who covered Mother Teresa's career for 27 years.

Something Beautiful for God by M Muggeridge (Harper & Row, 1971). The first book to bring Mother Teresa's work to the attention of readers in western countries.

The Love of Christ by G Goree and J Barbier (Collins, Fount Paperbacks, 1982). A selection from the writings and speeches of Mother Teresa.

We Do it for Jesus by E Le Joly (Darton Longman & Todd, 1977). An account of the work of the Missionaries of Charity.

Important Addresses

Co-Workers of Mother Teresa
c/o Missionaries of Charity
177 Bravington Road
London W9
England

Co-Workers of Mother Teresa
c/o Missionaries of Charity
St. Teresa's Church
Donore Avenue
Dublin 8
Ireland

Important Dates

1910 Born in Skopje.
1928 Travels to Ireland.
1929 Arrives in India.
1931 Takes first vows.
1937 Takes final vows; becomes headmistress of St. Mary's High School.
1946 Experiences "Day of Inspiration" (September 10).
1948 Leaves Loreto Order; takes nursing course at Patna; opens first slum school; becomes an Indian citizen.
1950 Establishes Congregation of the Missionaries of Charity; acquires 54A Lower Circular Road, Calcutta as Mother House.
1952 Opens home for the destitute dying (Nirmal Hriday).
1955 Opens Shishu Bhavan home for abandoned babies.
1957 Establishes medical services for lepers.
1960 Missionaries of Charity expand work beyond Calcutta.
1964 Raffles Pope's car and develops Shanti Nagar leper village.
1965 Opens center in Venezuela.
1968 Opens centers in Italy and Tanzania.
1970 Opens centers in Australia, Jordan and England; visits Skopje.
1973 Receives Templeton Prize.
1979 Wins Nobel Peace Prize.
1982 Visits Beirut on behalf of the Pope.
1984 Visits Bhopal pollution victims.
1988 Visits Armenian earthquake victims.

Glossary

Cholera A deadly water-borne disease, with a high risk of death.

Destitute Being in absolute poverty, on the edge of starvation.

Dispensary A clinic which gives out drugs and medicines.

Envoy A special messenger.

Hindu A follower of Hinduism — a group of religions with many gods, customs and festivals, which is widely found throughout India.

Humility To be modest and to realize that there are many people greater than oneself.

Immigrants Newcomers to a country in which they intend to live.

Missionary A person who chooses to spread knowledge about their religion, usually in a country where it is not well known.

Muslim A follower of the religion of Islam.

Novitiate A period of training for a nun before she takes her final vows; during this time she is known as a novice.

Refugee Someone who flees from their home to another place through fear of violence or some other threat.

31

Index

Picture Acknowledgements

The publishers would like to thank the following for providing the photographs in this book: Camera Press 4,8,10 (both), 11 (both), 12,13,14 (both), 15,16,18,19 (both), 20,21 (both), 22,23,24,25 (both), 27; Popperfoto Frontispiece, 26,28 (both); Yugoslav Tourist Board 6; Zefa 5.
The illustrations were provided by Malcolm Walker.